WHAT MACHINES DO
HAVING FUN

Written by John Allan
Illustrated by Esther Cuadrado

First published in 2022 by Hungry Tomato Ltd
F1, Old Bakery Studios, Blewetts Wharf, Malpas Road, Truro, Cornwall,
TR1 1QH, UK.

A CIP catalog record for this book is available from the British Library.

ISBN 978-1-914087-55-4

Manufactured in the USA

Discover more at
www.hungrytomato.com

CONTENTS

WHAT DO MACHINES DO FOR FUN?

Machines are everywhere, and they can be a lot of fun! From roller coasters to water scooters, life would be much more boring without them.

A DAY OUT WITH MACHINES

Some machines are hard at work so that we can relax and have fun. Some create amazing rides, games and activities. Others make tasty treats to enjoy along the way.

LET'S GET GOING!

Prepare to visit lots of busy machines that you might see on a fun day out. Take a look at them in action, then turn the page to discover what they do and how they work.

AT THE AMUSEMENT PARK

A trip to an amusement park can be a fun day out! There are lots of different rides to try out.

3
2
1

AT THE AMUSEMENT PARK

Roller coasters are the biggest and fastest rides at the park.

Carts zoom along the tracks at high speed. Some even flip upside down!

Roller coaster

This ride could make you very dizzy!

People sit inside teacups that spin round faster and faster!

Teacup Ride

These are little cars that you drive round a ring, trying to avoid the other cars.

Each car has a rubber edge that bounces off other cars.

Bumper cars

Merry-go-rounds play music as you go up and down, and round and round.

The horses move up and down, while the whole ride spins in a circle.

Merry-go-round

You can see for miles from the top of a Ferris wheel!

People sit in these cabins as the wheel spins round slowly.

Ferris Wheel

Prepare for a splash on this water ride.

Boats fall down a steep waterfall into a pool of water.

Log Flume

AT THE ARCADE

There are lots of fun games to play at the arcade, and they all work in different ways.

2

AT THE ARCADE

Two players follow the dance moves on the screen to see who's the best dancer.

The machine can tell when you step on the right square at the right time.

Dance Machine

This game can make it feel like you're riding a real motorcycle!

This screen shows a track for you to race on.

Motorcycle Simulator

There are lots of different types of video games, with different aims and rules.

They all have a screen to show the game, and controls to play it.

Arcade Video Game

This game tests your strength.

Boxing Machine

Punch this bag really hard to try and beat the highest score.

Win a prize by catching it in the claw.

Claw Machine

These controls move the claw around and tell it when to grab.

The aim of this game is to knock over all the bowling pins with a ball.

New balls are released here.

Bowling Alley

AT THE COFFEE SHOP

At this coffee shop, lots of tasty drinks and treats are made using machines.

AT THE COFFEE SHOP

This oven is used for baking tasty cakes and pastries.

Pastry Oven

Inside the oven can get very hot. These dials are used to set the perfect temperature.

A grill heats up sandwiches and makes them nice and crispy.

Sandwich Grill

Closing the lid presses two hot **grills** onto the top and bottom of the sandwich to heat it.

This machine can make different types of coffee.

This spout blows hot steam into milk to make it hot and frothy.

Coffee Machine

Dishwashers clean dirty plates, cups, glasses, and cutlery.

Dirty dishes are stored in trays inside the machine, ready to be washed.

Dishwasher

This grinds coffee beans into a powder to make coffee with.

The beans are poured into the top of the machine.

Coffee Grinder

Blenders are used to make drinks like milkshakes and smoothies.

Blender

Spinning blades at the bottom of the jug turn fruit and other ingredients to liquid.

AT THE BEACH

Nothing beats a sunny day at the beach! There are lots of brilliant boats and other machines to spot.

AT THE BEACH

This boat is powered by a motor. It can travel very fast.

It has a steering wheel to change direction.

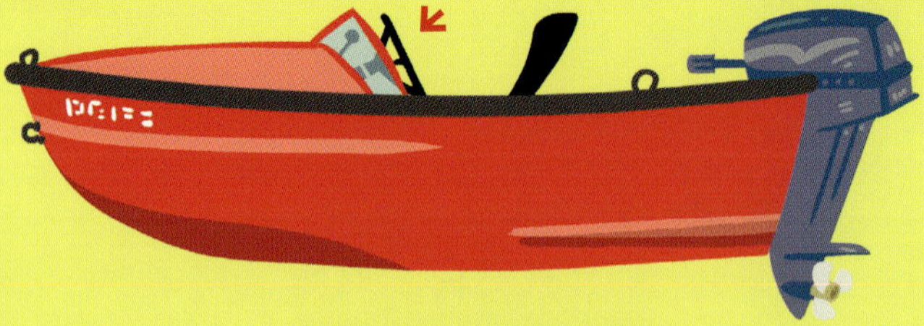

Motor Boat

Lifeboats are used to rescue people at sea.

The doors and windows are tightly sealed so no water can get in during storms.

Lifeboat

These vehicles speed along by pumping powerful jets of water out of the back.

Riders stand or sit on a water scooter, a bit like a motorcycle.

Water Scooter

Lighthouses warn boats about dangers in the water and guide them to shore.

Its bright light can be seen by boats a long way away.

Lighthouse

Ice cream can be a refreshing treat on a hot day.

Ice cream cart

This cart has a **freezer** inside to keep the ice cream frozen.

You can look through these to see far out to sea.

Put a coin in this slot to see through the **binoculars**.

Coin Operated Binoculars

FIND AND SEEK!

Can you find which machine each of these pictures are a part of?

1.

CLUE: You might get wet on this ride!

2.

CLUE: This machine has a bright light that can be seen by boats a long way away.

3.

CLUE: This machine is a game to see who's the best dancer.

4.

CLUE: This machine has two grills that heat up the sandwich.

5.

CLUE: This machine is used to cook yummy pastries and cakes.

6.

CLUE: This machine has a freezer inside.

7.

CLUE: This machine is a game where the aim is to knock over all the bowling pins with a ball.

8.

CLUE: This machine is the biggest and fastest ride at the amusement park.

DID YOU FIND THEM ALL?

Answers can be found on page 24.

GLOSSARY

Grills
Surfaces that can be heated up to cook food on.

Binoculars
A device that you look through with both eyes to see far away.

Motor
Part of a machine that makes something move. Similar to an engine.

Freezer
A machine that freezes food to keep it fresh or stop it from melting.

FIND AND SEEK ANSWERS

ANSWERS: 1. Log Flume, 2. Light House, 3. Dance Machine, 4. Sandwich Grill, 5. Pastry Oven, 6. Ice Cream Cart, 7. Bowling Alley, 8. Roller-Coaster.